MISSION
WASHINGTON, D.C.

Creator: Catherine Aragon ● Cover Designer: Nada Orlic
Content Editor: Sue Peterson

MISSION LOCATION: WASHINGTON, D.C.

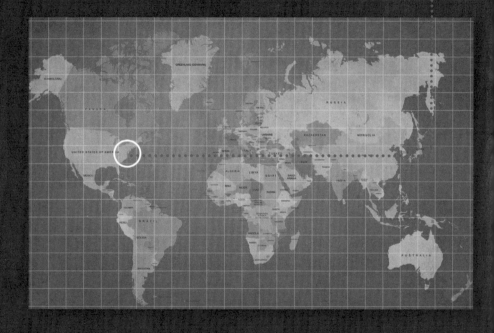

CONTENTS: *184*

AFTER COMPLETING EACH MISSION, CHECK (√) THE BOX AND WRITE THE NUMBER OF POINTS EARNED.

AT THE END, WRITE THE TOTAL NUMBER OF POINTS HERE:

ATTENTION: FUTURE SPECIAL AGENTS (YOU) AND CASE OFFICERS (GROWNUPS)

....

CONGRATULATIONS! THE SIA (SECRET INTERNATIONAL AGENCY) HAS SELECTED YOU AS A CANDIDATE TO BECOME A SPECIAL AGENT.

The SIA carries out important assignments, collecting intelligence in all corners of the globe. ("Intelligence" is spy-speak for "information.") Currently, we are in dire need of agents. Many want to join, but only a few have what it takes.

HOW WILL YOU PROVE YOU'RE READY TO JOIN THE MOST ELITE SPY AGENCY IN THE WORLD? You must complete a series of missions in Washington, D.C. Similar to a scavenger hunt (only better), these missions will require you to carry out challenging investigations and collect valuable intel (short for "intelligence"). For each mission, you'll earn points towards becoming a special agent.

YOUR ASSIGNMENT: TRAVEL TO D.C. WITH YOUR TEAM, LED BY YOUR CASE OFFICER. (A case officer accompanies agents on missions. Your case officer is your parent or other trusted adult.) You must earn at least 100 points to become a SIA special agent.

-The list of missions and the scorecard are on page 1.

-Read the "Anytime Missions" early, so that you'll remain on alert and ready to earn points.

-You don't need to complete all of the missions to reach 100 points or complete them in any particular order.

ATTENTION: GROWNUPS

Visit **scavengerhuntadventures.com/hunt** today to sign up for our email list and get these for your soon-to-be-agent:

• *The Museum Spy*: a free e-book

• A chance to win a **personalized copy** of any of our books especially for your agent (and even more **free** books!); Details online.

"I'm Signing Up Today."

MISSION RULES

- Be kind and respectful to team members.

- Your case officer (your parent or trusted adult) has the final decision regarding point awards.

- Your case officer serves as the official "scorekeeper."

- Your case officer has the final decision on what missions will be attempted. (Don't worry, you can still earn enough points to become an agent without completing all the missions.)

- Always be on alert. You never know when a chance to earn points lies just around the corner.

TO CONCEAL THEIR REAL IDENTITIES, SPECIAL AGENTS ALWAYS USE CODE NAMES. FOR EXAMPLE, JAMES BOND'S CODE NAME IS 007. THINK OF YOUR OWN CODE NAME TO USE DURING YOUR MISSION IN WASHINGTON, D.C.

SIGN YOUR CODE NAME HERE:

_____

DATE

IMPORTANT: FOR THE MISSIONS YOU WILL NEED A PEN OR PENCIL AND A CAMERA.

LET THE MISSIONS BEGIN – GOOD LUCK!

D.C. PRE-ARRIVAL BRIEF

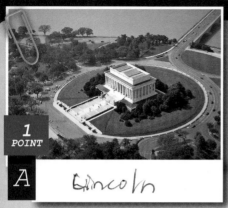

1 POINT

A Lincoln

1 POINT

Jefferson **B**

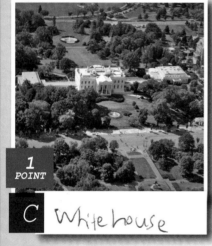

1 POINT

C Whitehouse

1 POINT

Cipital **D**

AGENTS MUST HAVE SHARP SKILLS WHEN IT COMES TO ANALYZING IMAGES, SUCH AS PHOTOGRAPHS, IN ORDER TO GATHER IMPORTANT INTEL. AERIAL PHOTOS LIKE THESE ARE TAKEN FROM HIGH IN THE SKY, FROM A PLANE, HELICOPTER, OR TALL BUILDING.

my notes:

_____

_____

First, examine these aerial photos of D.C. monuments. Next, study the photos of the same monuments taken at ground level (below).

☐ USING THE GROUND-LEVEL PHOTO AND THE MONUMENT'S DESCRIPTION, WRITE WHAT MONUMENT APPEARS IN EACH AERIAL PHOTO ON PAGE 4.

- **WHITE HOUSE**
  - Where the president lives and works
  - Surrounded by two "lawns": "North Lawn" and "South Lawn"

- **LINCOLN MEMORIAL**
  - Built in memory of President Abraham Lincoln
  - Square structure with columns on all sides

- **CAPITOL**
  - Meeting place of Congress; Dome connects House of Representatives and Senate sides

- **JEFFERSON MEMORIAL**
  - Constructed to honor President Thomas Jefferson
  - Rectangular "porch" leads to monument's dome

CAPITOL

IT'S CRITICAL THAT SPECIAL AGENTS PAY ATTENTION TO DETAILS, EVEN DETAILS AS TINY AS A SINGLE LETTER OF THE ALPHABET.

The capital of the U.S. is Washington, D.C. However, Congress (the Senate and the House of Representatives) meets in this building, the Capitol.

Outside the Capitol, from the reflecting pool

2 POINTS   ☐ **FIND THE 'STATUE OF FREEDOM.'**
Hint: Keep your head up.

1 POINT   ☐ **BONUS: ONCE INSIDE THE CAPITOL, FIND THE PLASTER MODEL CAST USED TO MAKE THE STATUE.**

Hunt down this statue of a Civil War general and president.

☑ **WHO IS THIS GENERAL?**
(Find his last name carved on the statue.)

2
POINTS

Taft

Inside the Capitol

☑ **FIND A STATUE OF THE SAME GENERAL AND PRESIDENT YOU JUST LOCATED OUTSIDE.**

2
POINTS

THE MYSTERY GENERAL/PRESIDENT

As you trek around inside, stay on alert and hunt down statues of:

2
POINTS
EACH

☑ **FREDERICK DOUGLASS** (A leader in the movement to abolish slavery)

☑ **ABRAHAM LINCOLN** (16th President who served during the Civil War)

☑ **ROSA PARKS** (Called the "First Lady of Civil Rights" and the "Mother of the Freedom Movement")

☐ **SAKAKAWEA** (A Shoshone who helped lead Lewis and Clark on their early-1800's expedition to explore the lands of the western U.S.)

☐ **JEANNETTE RANKIN** (First woman elected to Congress)

☑ **SEQUOYAH** (Inventor of the alphabet used by the Native American tribe, the Cherokee)

Hint: You'll find many of these in the National Statuary Hall, listed on page 9.

Rotunda

3
POINTS
☑ UNCOVER THIS IMAGE OF GEORGE WASHINGTON DEPICTED AS A GOD.

The Apotheosis of Washington represents the first president surrounded by figures from mythology like Liberty and Victoria.

3
POINTS
☑ TRACK DOWN THIS PAINTING OF THE FOUNDING FATHERS PRESENTING THE DECLARATION OF INDEPENDENCE.

1
POINT
☑ BONUS: FIND AN AMERICAN FLAG IN ONE OF THE ROTUNDA'S PAINTINGS.

Crypt

☑ **LOCATE THE STAR.** **2** *POINTS*

The city of Washington, D.C. is divided into four quadrants (Northeast, Northwest, Southeast, and Southwest). This star represents the very spot where they meet. If the star isn't roped off, have your photo snapped standing on top of it.

National Statuary Hall

☑ **FIND THE STATUE(S) FOR YOUR STATE.** **3** *POINTS*

(If you're not from the U.S., locate Hawaii's statue, King Kamehameha (*"Kah-may-huh-may-huh"*), the king and warrior from the 50th state.)

☑ **LOCATE THE STATUE ('LIBERTY') WITH TWO ANIMALS: AN EAGLE AND A SNAKE.** **3** *POINTS*

my notes:

....

....

....

SUPREME COURT

AS A SPECIAL AGENT, YOU MUST BE ABLE TO "HIDE IN PLAIN SIGHT." THAT MEANS BLENDING IN AND DOING WHAT OTHER TOURISTS DO: SNAPPING PHOTOS.

Hunt around outside the highest court in the country, the Supreme Court, for the next three items, taking a photo of each.

Outside

Track down these symbols of the Supreme Court and of justice.

2
POINTS

☑ **A SET OF SCALES** ....
These scales "weigh" the two sides of a case.

12 4

- SET OF SCALES
- BLINDFOLDED STATUE
- "LEX" INSCRIPTION
- JUSTICE STATUES
- JUSTICE BONUS

TOTAL POINTS

☑ **A STATUE WEARING A BLINDFOLD**

2 POINTS

Justice is supposed to be "blind." Because Justice (the statue) can't see, she judges objectively, without favoring one side or another.

☐ **"LEX" INSCRIPTION**

2 POINTS

"Lex" is the Latin word for "law." Latin was the language of Ancient Rome, a society dating back many centuries that influenced how our courts operate today.

Inside

FIND THE STATUES OF THESE JUSTICES:

☐ **JOHN MARSHALL**

2 POINTS

(The fourth Chief Justice)

☐ **SANDRA DAY O'CONNOR**

2 POINTS

(The first female Justice)

BONUS:

☐ WHO WAS THE FIRST AFRICAN AMERICAN JUSTICE?

1 POINT

☐ WHO WAS THE FIRST HISPANIC AMERICAN JUSTICE?

1 POINT

my notes:

....

AIR & SPACE MUSEUM

HIGH UP IN THE SKY ... THIS HAS PROVEN TO BE ONE OF THE BEST PLACES FROM WHICH TO SPY. GOVERNMENTS USE SATELLITES (MACHINES THAT ORBIT THE EARTH TAKING PICTURES) AND OTHER FORMS OF AIRCRAFT TO SPY AND TO GATHER INFORMATION. WHO KNOWS — A SATELLITE COULD BE SNAPPING PICTURES OF THE MUSEUM AS YOU READ THIS!

As you trek through the museum, remain on alert and hunt down these historical objects.

- U-2C
- UAVS
- SPIRIT OF SAINT LOUIS
- APOLLO 11 & MOON ROCK
- WRIGHT FLYER
- SPIRIT OF FREEDOM
- 5B VEGA

☐ LOCKHEED U-2C

2 POINTS

A stealth aircraft the U.S. used in top secret operations to spy on its former arch enemy, the Soviet Union.

☑ MILITARY UNMANNED AERIAL VEHICLES

2 POINTS

With such names as "Dark Star," "Dragon Eye," "Predator," and "Shadow," these aircraft (a.k.a. "UAV" or a "drone"), as their name implies, aren't flown by pilots (they're "unmanned"). They are operated either by remote control or on-board computers.

my notes:

....

....

....

☑ SPIRIT OF SAINT LOUIS

2
POINTS

Charles Lindbergh completed the first solo non-stop flight across the Atlantic Ocean in this plane, traveling from Long Island, New York to Paris. The date: May 21, 1927. Nowadays this flight would take around eight hours; back then it took 33 hours, 30 minutes.

2
POINTS

☑ APOLLO 11 COMMAND MODULE COLUMBIA

Apollo 11 flew astronauts Neil Armstrong, Edwin "Buzz" Aldrin, and Michael Collins to the Moon in July 1969, where Armstrong and Aldrin became the first humans to set foot on the Moon.

1
POINT

☑ BONUS: TOUCH THE MOON ROCK.

☑ **1903 WRIGHT FLYER** `2 POINTS`

☐ **BUD LIGHT SPIRIT OF FREEDOM** `2 POINTS`

This balloon flew a complete voyage around the world in two weeks in 2002, and its pilot became the first person to complete a solo flight around the world in a balloon.

☐ **WHO WAS THE PILOT?** `1 POINT`

☑ **AMELIA EARHART'S 5B VEGA** `2 POINTS`

☐ **BONUS: WHAT'S THE PLANE'S ID NUMBER?** `1 POINT`

Hint: It's two letters and four numbers.

Amelia Earhart became the first woman to fly solo non-stop across the Atlantic Ocean and after that across the U.S. She completed these journeys in this plane.

NATIONAL ARCHIVES

SPECIAL AGENTS ALWAYS NEED TO HAVE THEIR EYES PEELED FOR INTELLIGENCE: CLUES AND CRITICAL INFORMATION THAT OTHERS OFTEN MISS. CAN YOU FIND THE 'INTEL' NEEDED TO COMPLETE THIS MISSION?

Outside

2
POINTS

☑ FIND THE INSCRIPTION, "WHAT IS PAST IS PROLOGUE."

A "prologue" serves as an introduction to a play or a book. The monument's designers took this quote from a work by the famous British

- "WHAT IS PAST…" INSCRIPTION
- TWO STATUES' INSCRIPTIONS
- TWO EAGLES
- DOCUMENT EXCERPTS
- SIGNATURES OF JOHN HANCOCK AND GEORGE WASHINGTON

Shakespeare

playwright William Shakespeare. It reminds us that history sets the stage for the present. Housed here you'll uncover some of the most important documents in U.S. history, which have set the stage for our country's present and future.

☑ HUNT DOWN THE TWO STATUES ABOVE. WHAT DO THEIR INSCRIPTIONS READ?

2
POINTS

my notes:

....

....

....

NATIONAL ARCHIVES

2 POINTS ☑ TRACK DOWN TWO EAGLES LIKE THIS ONE PERCHED ON THE BUILDING, WITH THEIR BACKS TO EACH OTHER.

Inside

The documents resting inside date from the late 1700's and require sharp eyes (like those of a spy-in-training) for proper analysis. These three images are snapshots of excerpts of the Archives' three most important documents.

3 POINTS ☑ MATCH THESE TO THE ORIGINAL DOCUMENTS.

☑ **FIND JOHN HANCOCK'S SIGNATURE ON THE DECLARATION OF INDEPENDENCE.**

`1 POINT`

(It appears similar to the signature above, but faded.)

Hancock, who served as president of the Continental Congress, was the first to sign the *Declaration*. His large signature stood out so much that the term "John Hancock" became another term for "signature." Sign your "John Hancock" here (using your special agent name, of course).

....

☑ **LOCATE GEORGE WASHINGTON'S SIGNATURE ON THE CONSTITUTION.**

`1 POINT`

MUSEUM OF NATURAL HISTORY

ONE OF THE TOP RULES OF SPYING: BLEND IN WITH YOUR SURROUNDINGS. YOU CAN NEVER SPOT THE BEST AGENTS BECAUSE THEY DON'T *LOOK* LIKE AGENTS. HERE, THAT MEANS "PLAYING TOURIST" BY STROLLING AROUND THE MUSEUM (AND TAKING A FEW PHOTOS).

1 POINT EACH Find these objects (1 point each):

☑ TIGER   ☑ DINGO   ☐ TAYRA   ☑ POLAR BEAR

- ANIMAL SEARCH
- CROWN OF THORNS
- SHARK JAWS & PHOTO
- ANIMAL BONES
- CAT MUMMY
- GEM SEARCH

11

TOTAL POINTS

☐ **CROWN OF THORNS**

1 POINT

☑ **GIANT GREAT WHITE SHARK JAWS**

1 POINT

These huge chompers from a shark that lived millions of years ago are surrounded by protective glass.

☑ **BONUS: HAVE YOUR PHOTO SNAPPED STANDING ON THE OTHER SIDE OF THE GLASS, SURROUNDED BY THE JAWS.***

1 POINT

Stand on one side of the glass and have a teammate stand on the other with a camera. Have the teammate stand back a bit so that you and the jaws fit in the viewfinder.

☑ **WHICH ANIMAL BONES DID YOU FIND THE CREEPIEST?**

1 POINT

squid

☐ **HUNT DOWN THE CAT MUMMY.**

1 POINT

☐ **FIND THE DOM PEDRO AQUAMARINE.**

1 POINT

☑ **LOCATE THE HOPE DIAMOND.**

1 POINT

my notes:

....

....

*(If the camera flash gets in the way, then stand beside the glass case.) Would you fit inside the jaws?

MUSEUM OF AMERICAN HISTORY

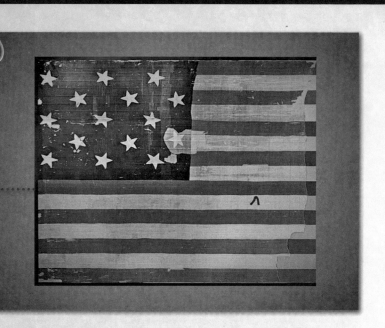

SPIES NEED A "COVER": A GO-TO GIG THAT "COVERS" THEIR REAL MISSION. WHILE YOU MAY BE AN AGENT-IN-TRAINING, REMEMBER YOUR "COVER" AS A TOURIST. TIME TO START PLAYING TOURIST BY EXPLORING A MUSEUM AND TRACKING DOWN:

2 POINTS ☑ THE 200-YEAR-OLD FLAG THAT INSPIRED THE STAR SPANGLED BANNER

1 POINT ☑ WHO WROTE THE LINES OF THE STAR SPANGLED BANNER (OUR NATIONAL ANTHEM)?

Francis Scott Key

☐ JOHN BULL LOCOMOTIVE **2** POINTS

☑ BENJAMIN FRANKLIN'S CANE **2** POINTS

☐ BONUS: FRANKLIN HANDED DOWN THIS CANE TO WHICH AMERICAN PRESIDENT? **1** POINT

BENJAMIN FRANKLIN

☑ GROUP OF FOUR DINER CHAIRS **2** POINTS

☐ WHAT IS THE NAME OF THIS EXHIBIT? **1** POINT

American Stories

☐ WHAT DATE DID THE SIT-IN AT THE LUNCH COUNTER START? **1** POINT

1963

my notes:

☑ **DOROTHY'S RUBY RED SLIPPERS FROM 'THE WIZARD OF OZ'**

☐ **THOMAS JEFFERSON'S PORTABLE DESK**

(If Jefferson had lived today he probably would've used a laptop computer for writing, but back in 1776 this Founding Father used this self-designed portable desk for penning the *Declaration of Independence*.)

☐ **ABRAHAM LINCOLN'S HAT**

(Lincoln donned this top hat the night of April 14, 1865, when he was assassinated at Washington D.C.'s Ford Theater by an actor named John Wilkes Booth.)

☐ **BILL CLINTON'S SAXOPHONE**

☑ MICHELLE OBAMA'S INAUGURAL GOWN

2 POINTS

(She wore this gown at the 2009 Inaugural Ball for her husband Barack Obama, the nation's first African American president.)

☐ STUBBY

2 POINTS

Stubby received many medals for his bravery during the 17 battles he served in World War I. Stubby's owner, an Army soldier, secretly brought Stubby with him and the two shipped out to Europe for war. Stubby even helped capture an enemy spy by attacking the spy and biting him until backup (American soldiers) arrived. Stubby achieved the rank of sergeant before returning home and eventually serving as the mascot of the Georgetown University Hoyas.

☑ WHAT THREE OBJECTS DID YOU FIND THE MOST UNUSUAL?

3 POINTS

tot phone, whanpam, big clock, cananball punch bowl

☐ WHAT THREE OBJECTS DID YOU FIND THE MOST IMPORTANT TO AMERICAN HISTORY?

3 POINTS

my notes: *star spangled banner, Washington's uniform, atomic bomb, hervey helicopter*

WHITE HOUSE

The home and workplace of **"POTUS"** (the **President of the United States**) has over 130 rooms. Here, the president and staff meet with foreign dignitaries, military leaders, members of Congress, and business leaders to make decisions about the most important national and global issues.

The White House from Lafayette Square

1600 _____ Avenue: this is the official address of the White House. The street is named after a U.S. state that begins with "P."

11

TOTAL POINTS

- ADDRESS
- WHITE HOUSE PHOTOS (2)
- DOLLAR BILL
- LAFAYETTE SQUARE PRESIDENT
- ZERO MILESTONE INSCRIPTIONS

☑ LOCATE A STREET SIGN WITH THE STATE NAME FOR THE ANSWER. *Pennsylvania*

2 POINTS

☐ HAVE YOUR PHOTO SNAPPED WITH THE WHITE HOUSE IN THE BACKGROUND.

2 POINTS

☑ BONUS: BEFORE LEAVING D.C., FIND OUT WHICH DOLLAR BILL HAS AN IMAGE OF THE WHITE HOUSE PRINTED ON THE BACK. *20*

1 POINT

Across the street from the White House stands Lafayette Square, named for the French general Marquis de Lafayette (Marquis = "Mar-kee"), who helped the Americans defeat the British in the Revolutionary War. Statues of war heroes from foreign lands dot the park (including Lafayette himself). You'll also find a statue of one American. This war hero served as president, and his image is printed on the front of a dollar bill, the same dollar bill with the White House printed on the back.

☑ WHO IS THIS PRESIDENT?

2 POINTS

Alexander Hamelton

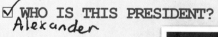

The President

Lafayette

The White House from the National Mall

Venture to the National Mall for another prime view of the president's residence.

2 **POINTS** ☐ HAVE YOUR PHOTO SNAPPED IN FRONT OF THIS OTHER SIDE OF THE WHITE HOUSE.

Hunt down the "Zero Milestone."

EXAMINE THE SIDES AND FIND WHICH SIDE (N, S, E, OR W) CONTAINS THESE INSCRIPTIONS:

☐ **"ZERO MILESTONE"**

1 POINT

☐ **"POINT FOR THE MEASUREMENT OF DISTANCES FROM WASHINGTON ON HIGHWAYS OF THE UNITED STATES"**

1 POINT

The Zero Milestone was meant to serve as the starting milestone for all road distances in the country. Now though, only road distances in the D.C. area are measured from it.

my notes:

....

....

WASHINGTON MONUMENT

This monument may honor America's first president, George Washington, but it certainly is the monument of "5's": it stands 555 and 5 1/8 inches tall, measures 55 feet wide, and was recently reopened following the repairs from a 5.8 magnitude earthquake that struck in 2011.

1 POINT ☑ EXAMINE THE OUTSIDE AND LOCATE THE SPOT ON THE TOWER WHERE THE MARBLE STONE CHANGES COLOR.

The monument's first stone was laid on July 4, 1848. Building continued as scheduled for six years, but money for the construction dried up. Then, the Civil War broke out. When building finally began again in 1876, builders used stones from a different quarry.

The stones looked close enough at first, but after weather, pollution, and time took their toll, the difference was obvious and it was way too late to change the stones.

We have different reports on how many U.S. flags surround the monument: some say 50, others say 56.

☐ **HOW MANY FLAGS DO YOU COUNT?**

50

1
POINT

Inside

☐ **SPOT THESE MONUMENTS FROM THE TOP:**
(Don't worry, if the elevator malfunctions, which it has in the past, it's *only* a 897-step climb!)

1
POINT EACH

● **CAPITOL**   ● **SMITHSONIAN CASTLE**

● **JEFFERSON MEMORIAL**   ● **WHITE HOUSE**

GEORGE WASHINGTON: AMERICA'S FIRST SPYMASTER

Washington, a.k.a. Agent 711

Tallmadge, a.k.a. John Bolton

The year: 1776, America was in the midst of war with Great Britain, the mightiest empire in the world, which had a stronghold on the important port city of New York. How could George Washington hope to get his hands on the valuable intel he needed to help him defeat the British? **Spies, of course.**

Under direct orders from Washington, Benjamin Tallmadge managed The Culper Ring, a spy ring whose name Washington devised from nearby Culpeper County, Virginia.

Agents put their lives on the line and obtained **top-secret intel** about Britain's war plans. They **smuggled intel across enemy lines** using all sorts of spy-craft techniques like INVISIBLE INK and **secret codes.** Some of the agents were **beyond top-secret:** not even Washington himself knew the identities of some of the members.

The Culper Ring passed along messages using secret codes, like the one below which the agents used for masking numbers.

☑ USE THE CODE TO FIGURE OUT THE DAY AND YEAR OF THE BRITISH SURRENDER AT YORKTOWN, VIRGINIA WHICH ENDED THE REVOLUTIONARY WAR.

2 POINTS

DATE: OCTOBER-EQ-ENOE DECODED: OCTOBER -19 -1781

TOP SECRET
1 2 3 4 5 6 7 8 9 0

KOREAN VETS MEMORIAL.

5

TOTAL POINTS

WAR LOCATION

D.C.

Track down the troop statues on patrol inside the triangle. Next, look to the reflective wall.

☑ **COUNT THE TOTAL TROOPS YOU SEE IN THE TRIANGLE *AND* IN THE WALL'S REFLECTION.**

3
POINTS

This number represents the _14_ th Parallel. (_19_ = the total number of troops you see.) This line of latitude marked the border between North Korea and South Korea (the two "Koreas" battling at war). The U.S. backed South Korea during this war (1950-1953), where 54,246 Americans died. It ended with no true winner or loser. Today, this parallel passes through the Korean border and through this monument.

☑ **TRACK DOWN THE FINAL WORD IN THIS PHRASE IN SILVER LETTERS: "FREEDOM IS NOT** _free_ **."**

2
POINTS

This saying shows appreciation for the military members who give up so much (sometimes their own lives) to protect freedom.

WORLD WAR II MEMORIAL

This memorial honors the 16 million who served during World War II, the over 400,000 who lost their lives, and the millions who supported the war effort from home.

World War II involved nearly every region of the world. The Axis Powers (led by Germany, Italy, and Japan) battled the Allied Powers (led by the United States, France, Great Britain, Russia, and China).

23

TOTAL POINTS

- MILITARY SERVICE SEALS
- PILLARS: COUNT & HOME STATE PHOTO
- ARCHES INSCRIPTION
- WAR YEARS
- PEARL HARBOR AND D-DAY: DATES & RELIEF
- FACTORY RELIEF
- FREEDOM WALL

☑ **UNCOVER THE MILITARY SERVICE SEALS IN THE CENTRAL PLAZA.**

3 POINTS

(Note: Together with the military seals, you will also find the Merchant Marine seal.)

☑ **HOW MANY PILLARS CIRCLE THE FOUNTAIN?**

2 POINTS

56

Each pillar has an inscription of one of the names of the 48 U.S. states, the District of Columbia, the territories of Alaska and Hawaii, and the Commonwealth of the Philippines, Puerto Rico, Guam, American Samoa, or the U.S. Virgin Islands.
(All with their 1945 status.)

☑ **HAVE YOUR PHOTO SNAPPED WITH YOUR HOME'S PILLAR IN THE BACKGROUND.**

2 POINTS

(If you're not from the U.S., adopt Washington D.C. as your temporary home.)

my notes:

....

....

2 POINTS

Ⓐ **WHAT TWO WORDS ARE INSCRIBED ON THE TWO LARGE ARCHES?**

atlantic pacific

U.S. forces fought in two military areas on opposite sides of the world. Ships crisscrossed the Atlantic, transporting service members to Northern Africa and Europe to fight against the Nazis and Italians. Meanwhile in the Pacific American units battled the Japanese.

2 POINTS

☑ **FOR THE U.S., THE WAR LASTED FROM 19_41_ TO 19_45_.**

Hunt down this design set into the floor of the monument, with the two years next to it.

In 1939 after Germany invaded Poland, France and the United Kingdom declared war on Germany, thereby officially beginning World War II. However, for the U.S. the war began when the Japanese attacked our military bases at Pearl Harbor, Hawaii.

☑ **THIS SURPRISE ATTACK OCCURRED ON:**
Dec _7_, 19_41_.

2 POINTS

To find the answer, locate an inscription of a speech by President Franklin D. Roosevelt.

ROOSEVELT

These very words of Roosevelt's address Americans heard broadcast over the airwaves. As people all over the country gathered in front of their radios, they learned of the Pearl Harbor bombing and realized that **the country was on the brink of entering the war**.

☐ **FIND THE RELIEF* SHOWING A FAMILY ···. LISTENING TO ROOSEVELT'S ADDRESS.**

2 POINTS

☐ **WHAT DATE WAS D-DAY?**

2 POINTS

EISENHOWER

Locate the answer in an inscription from a speech by General Dwight D. Einsenhower.

*Relief = a flat sculpture

☑ HUNT DOWN THE D-DAY RELIEF.

2 POINTS

Arriving via sea and air, 160,000 Allied soldiers (including 73,000 Americans) stormed onto the beaches in Normandy, France this very day, stunning the evil Nazis with a massive attack. Thanks to their bravery the Allies managed to push forward into France, save Europe from the Nazis, and eventually win the war.

☑ FIND THE AIRPLANE CONSTRUCTION RELIEF.

2 POINTS

See the woman in the center of the relief? With the men away fighting, American women took to the factories to help build planes like these and produce ammunition that the troops used to win the war.

my notes:

....

....

....

☑ FIND THE MESSAGE: "HERE WE MARK THE PRICE OF FREEDOM."

This message lies next to the "Freedom Wall," a wall shining with over 4,000 gold stars, each one representing 100 Americans who died or remained missing in the war.

MARTIN LUTHER KING, JR. MEMORIAL

In 1963 Dr. Martin Luther King, Jr. gave his famous "I Have a Dream" speech during the March on Washington, where he spoke about the dream he had that his children would live in a country where they weren't judged on the color of their skin, but instead on their character*.

The monument stands at _ _ _ _ Independence Avenue, S.W.

The digits in the address are the same year the Civil Rights Act became law and King won the Nobel Peace Prize.

2 POINTS ☐ TRACK DOWN THE QUOTE ON THE NEXT PAGE INSCRIBED IN THE MONUMENT (PART OF KING'S NOBEL PRIZE ACCEPTANCE SPEECH).

*character = a person's fairness and honesty

TOTAL POINTS

The quote begins, "I believe that unarmed truth ..."

☐ **WHAT IS THE YEAR?**

1
POINT

(Below the quote you'll find this important year and the street number.)

MARCH ON WASHINGTON

MARTIN LUTHER &
CORETTA SCOTT KING

☑ **LOCATE THE INSCRIPTION, THAT BEGINS "OUT OF THE MOUNTAIN OF DESPAIR..."**

2
POINTS

This above quote inspired the "Stone of Hope" sculpture. It gets its name from King's "I Have a Dream" speech.

my notes:

....

....

....

KING WITH PRESIDENT LYNDON
JOHNSON AND CIVIL RIGHTS LEADERS
AT THE WHITE HOUSE

Look at the two huge stones you walked between to
enter the monument. They represent the "Mountain
of Despair" in King's speech. The towering stone
where King stands symbolizes the "Stone of
Hope." Here, King has managed to break away from
"despair" and looks out over the horizon with the
vision that one day all Americans will be treated
equally.

2
POINTS

☑ SNAP A PHOTO OF KING AND THE STONE OF
HOPE, WITH THE MOUNTAIN OF DESPAIR IN
THE BACKGROUND.

my notes:

....

....

A Chinese master sculptor created the huge statue of Dr. King. Compare this mission's photos of Dr. King with the statue's face.

KING ANSWERS QUESTIONS FROM THE PRESS

☑ **IN YOUR OPINION, DID THE ARTIST DO A GOOD JOB PORTRAYING KING?**

3 POINTS

Find the inscription that begins, "We shall overcome..."

☐ **WHAT YEAR DID KING SPEAK THESE WORDS?**

2 POINTS

(Below the quote you'll find the year.)

Dr. King's life was under constant threat. He was assassinated in the year you just found in Memphis, Tennessee.

my notes:

....

....

43

LINCOLN MEMORIAL

SPECIAL AGENTS MUST BE IN TIP-TOP SHAPE, WHETHER THAT MEANS SPRINTING TO MAKE A FAST GETAWAY OR REMAINING ON ALERT WHILE EXPLORING ALL CORNERS OF MONUMENTS LIKE THIS ONE TO COMPLETE A MISSION.

Abraham Lincoln, the 16th president, served during the Civil War, a war that lasted four long years (1861-1865) where 620,000 soldiers died in battle. (That's about the population of all of Washington, D.C.)

Inside the monument

2
POINTS

☑ FIND "CIVIL WAR" INSCRIBED TWICE ON THE WALLS.

14

TOTAL POINTS

- CIVIL WAR INSCRIPTION
- EMANCIPATION PROCLAMATION DATE
- LINCOLN ASSASSINATION YEAR
- LINCOLN'S DOLLAR AND COIN
- 'I HAVE A DREAM' INSCRIPTION
- ILLINOIS INSCRIPTION
- PHOTO ILLUSION

☑ LINCOLN ISSUED THE EMANCIPATION PROCLAMATION ON WHAT DATE?

2 POINTS

1862

To find the answer, hunt around in the visitor center for a plaque that begins, "A proclamation…"

The *Emancipation Proclamation* was an order that freed the slaves in the Confederate States. Soon after Lincoln's *Emancipation Proclamation* came the 13th Amendment to the *Constitution* which would free all slaves.

• •

The man on the left, Lincoln's head of the Union Intelligence Service (a.k.a. "spy chief") and former private eye, foiled an attempt to assassinate the president in 1861. He went deep undercover to discover plots of angry Southerners to kill Lincoln, a president they were furious with for wanting to abolish slavery. Unfortunately Lincoln didn't escape another attempt made on his life.

Allan Pinkerton, President Lincoln, 1862

☑ HE WAS ASSASSINATED (BY A MAN NAMED JOHN WILKES BOOTH) IN WHAT YEAR?

2 POINTS

1865

my notes:

....

....

1 POINT ☑ BONUS: ABRAHAM LINCOLN APPEARS ON WHICH U.S. DOLLAR AND COIN?

penny, $5

Outside the monument

☑ FIND THIS INSCRIPTION. **2** POINTS

From this very spot Dr. Martin Luther King, Jr. gave his famous "I Have a Dream" speech, where he preached about the importance of equality for all Americans. Imagine standing here, the National Mall filled with an audience of 250,000 people listening to your every word.

☑ TRACK DOWN "ILLINOIS" INSCRIBED ALONG THE TOP OF THE MONUMENT. **2** POINTS

Lincoln served as a congressman from Illinois before being elected president.

IN THE WORLD OF SPECIAL AGENTS, NOTHING IS WHAT IT SEEMS. WHAT APPEARS TO BE YOUR EVERYDAY CLOCK IS REALLY A VIDEO CAMERA. WHAT SEEMS TO BE AN ORDINARY KID VACATIONING IN D.C. IS REALLY A SPECIAL-AGENT-IN-TRAINING (YOU!). THE SAME GOES FOR PHOTOGRAPHS: THINGS AREN'T ALWAYS AS THEY APPEAR.

Take a look at this photo. It appears as if the person has fit the Washington Monument between two fingers. To create this illusion, face the Washington Monument, hold up your thumb and index finger of your left hand in the shape of a "C." Have someone on your team stand next to you on your right side with a camera and have this person adjust your hand until the monument appears to fit between your fingers.

☐ TAKE A PHOTO OF THE WASHINGTON MONUMENT FITTING BETWEEN YOUR FINGERS.

3
POINTS

VIETNAM VETS MEMORIAL.

This memorial pays tribute to the over 58,000 American service members killed or missing-in-action (MIA) in the Vietnam War. Tens of thousands of names are inscribed on the dark reflective wall, where you may see flowers or American flags left in remembrance of friends and family members lost during the war.

2 POINTS ☑ **FIND THE YEARS "1959" AND "1975" INSCRIBED ON THE WALL.**

Service member names are listed in chronological order, starting with 1959 and ending, almost 20 long years and 58,000 names later, at 1975 (the year the war finally ended).

5

TOTAL POINTS

Locate the bronze statue of three soldiers. Face the front of the statue and examine the soldier with the towel around his neck.

☑ **WHAT ELSE HANGS AROUND HIS NECK, LYING AGAINST HIS CHEST?** *dog tags*

1 POINT

Each soldier would have been given a set of these which had imprinted the soldier's name, social security number, blood type, and religion.

SOLDIERS IN VIETNAM

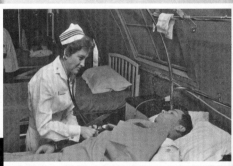

☑ **LOCATE THE VIETNAM WOMEN'S MEMORIAL.**

2 POINTS

(Dedicated to women who served in the Vietnam War; many women served as nurses)

my notes:

JEFFERSON MEMORIAL.

ALL THE SPY GEAR AND TOP SECRET INTEL IN THE WORLD WON'T HELP YOU IF YOU DON'T HAVE A MIND LIKE A STEEL TRAP. LET'S TEST YOUR SKILLS AT THIS MONUMENT HONORING THE THIRD PRESIDENT.

FIND THESE QUOTES FROM THE DECLARATION OF INDEPENDENCE:

1
POINT

☐ "WE SOLEMNLY PUBLISH AND DECLARE THAT THESE COLONIES ARE AND OF RIGHT OUGHT TO BE FREE AND INDEPENDENT STATES."

1
POINT

☐ "WE HOLD THESE TRUTHS TO BE SELF-EVIDENT: THAT ALL MEN ARE CREATED EQUAL."

5

- DECLARATION OF INDEPENDENCE QUOTES
- INSCRIPTION SPELLING
- DATE JEFFERSON DIED

TOTAL POINTS

Jefferson's *Declaration* was supposed to be inscribed correctly in the monument. However, the monument's inscriptions contain a few errors: among them being a misspelled word from the *Declaration* excerpt below.

We hold these truths to be self-evident, that all men are created equal, that they are endowed by their Creator with certain unalienable Rights,

☐ **WHAT WORD IS SPELLED DIFFERENTLY IN THE DECLARATION EXCERPT VS. IN THE EXCERPT'S INSCRIPTION?**

1 POINT

....

☐ **WHAT AGE WAS JEFFERSON WHEN HE DIED?**

2 POINTS

Hint: Somewhere in the monument, uncover the year he was born and the year he died. Subtract these for the answer.

Thomas Jefferson died on Independence Day (July 4), on the fiftieth anniversary of the signing of the *Declaration of Independence*.

FDR Memorial

Roosevelt as a young man

Before you stands a memorial to one of our greatest presidents: Franklin D. Roosevelt. **Can you find the "intel" to complete this mission?**

2 ☐ **FIND ROOSEVELT SEATED NEXT TO A RADIO.**
POINTS

In the 1930's and 40's Americans gathered in front of radios like this to learn the latest news from the president on important events - like the Great Depression and America's fate in a world war.

2 ☐ **FIND THE PHRASE "I HATE WAR" CARVED INTO**
POINTS
EACH **LARGE STONES. (FOUR POINTS MAX)**

What war did Roosevelt lead the nation through?

12

TOTAL POINTS

- RADIO
- 'I HATE WAR' INSCRIPTIONS
- BREAD LINE STATUES
- PRESIDENTIAL PET
- ELEANOR ROOSEVELT STATUE

☑ **HOW MANY STATUES WAIT IN LINE TO BUY BREAD (LIKE THE PEOPLE IN THIS PHOTO)?** *3*

2 POINTS

Roosevelt led the nation through the Great Depression, a time when Americans were out of work and some so poor they couldn't afford food (like bread) and had to wait in line for food from charities.

☐ **HAVE YOUR PHOTO TAKEN BY THE PRESIDENTIAL PET - A TERRIER NAMED "FALA."**

2 POINTS

☑ **FIND THE STATUE OF ELEANOR ROOSEVELT.**

Instead of simply attending events at her husband's side the way First Ladies had in the past, Eleanor Roosevelt wanted something more. She used her position to stand up for the rights of women, African-Americans, and the poor. She traveled across the country to learn how Americans fared through the Great Depression.

2 POINTS

She even traveled to Europe to visit the troops fighting in World War II. She then served in the United Nations, where she fought for human rights in the hope that people around the world would someday all be treated fairly.

ANYTIME MISSIONS

....

THE BEST AGENTS HAVE A HIGH LEVEL OF
SOMETHING CALLED "SITUATIONAL AWARENESS."
THESE QUICK-WITTED AGENTS PAY CLOSE
ATTENTION TO THEIR SURROUNDINGS — READY TO
COLLECT CRITICAL INTELLIGENCE AND RESPOND
TO DANGEROUS SITUATIONS. HAVING EXCELLENT
"SITUATIONAL AWARENESS" (SA FOR SHORT)
MEANS ALWAYS BEING "ON ALERT."

These missions will test your SA. You can complete
these at any time during your stay. Don't let your
guard down, or you may miss a chance to win points.

....

Hunt down a Washington, D.C. license plate and at
the bottom find the city's slogan.

☑ WHAT IS THE SLOGAN? **2** POINTS

Taxation without representation

D.C. residents, like other U.S. residents, must
pay taxes to the federal government. However,
D.C.'s representative in the House of
Representatives can't actually vote in Congress.
Their representative doesn't have full power to
"represent" D.C. residents, but the residents
must still pay taxes. So, the city adopted this
slogan.

SEE WINDOW STICKER • WASHINGTON, DC • SEE WINDOW STICKER

CT ≡ ★★★ 0255

my notes:

....

....

HUNT DOWN A SOUVENIR FROM EACH OF THE CITY'S SPORTS TEAMS.

1 POINT EACH

1 point for each item from each team, seven points max

☑ NATIONALS (BASEBALL)

☐ SPIRIT (WOMEN'S SOCCER)

☑ REDSKINS (FOOTBALL)

☐ WIZARDS (BASKETBALL)

☐ MYSTICS (WOMEN'S BASKETBALL)

☑ CAPITALS (HOCKEY)

☐ D.C. UNITED (SOCCER)

ANYTIME MISSIONS: BONUS

Come across a monument or exhibit that's closed? Not enough time in D.C. to reach 100 points? Have no fear, use these missions to achieve your goal. Your case officer sets the points.

 ☑ **FIND THE MOTTO "E PLURIBUS UNUM."**

"E Pluribus Unum": This is a "motto" of the U.S. It's a Latin phrase (Latin was the language of Ancient Rome) which means "Out of many, one." It symbolizes the many states (or former colonies) that came together to form a single nation, and it means that people from different religions, races, and backgrounds come together to form one United States. Stay on point in the city and find this motto on buildings, statues, paintings, and even on coins.

*To receive each point, the motto must be on a different kind of item. For example, once you have found it on a type of coin, then that's all the points for the motto on that type of coin.

 ☑ **RIDE D.C.'S SUBWAY: THE METRO.**

 ☑ **PLAN YOUR TEAM'S METRO ROUTES TOGETHER WITH YOUR CASE OFFICER.**

THE FINAL MISSION

Mission complete? Great! Case officers, please visit **Scavengerhuntadventures.Com/hunt**. (All lowercase letters.)

"I'm Signing Up Today."

☐ **SIGN UP FOR OUR EMAIL LIST TO GET:**

• *The Museum Spy*: a free e-book

• A chance to win a **personalized copy** of any of our books printed especially for your agent (and even more **free** books!); Details online.

☐ **CLICK 'SPECIAL AGENT CERTIFICATES'** For a personalized certificate for your new agent!

GREAT FOR GROUP TRIPS

We offer **special multi-copy pricing** and **personalized books** - great for field trips and group trips. Visit **Scavengerhuntadventures.Com/groups** for more info.

PLEASE HELP SPREAD THE WORD

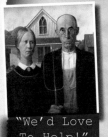

"We'd Love To Help!"

We're a small family business and would be thrilled if you **left a review online*** or recommended our books to a friend.

OUR BOOKS
Paris, London, Amsterdam, Rome, New York, D.C., Barcelona, St. Augustine - more on the way!

*We can't mention the site name here, but it begins with "AM"!

ANSWER KEY

ONCE A FINAL ANSWER IS SUBMITTED, YOUR CASE OFFICER CAN CHECK IT HERE. IF YOU PEEK AT THIS ANSWER KEY BEFORE SUBMITTING YOUR FINAL ANSWER, YOU WON'T RECEIVE ANY POINTS FOR THAT QUESTION.

Pre-Arrival Brief: A:Lincoln Memorial, B:Jefferson Memorial, C:White House, D:Capitol

#1 Capitol:

-The general: Ulysses Grant

#2 Supreme Court: -Bonus: Thurgood Marshall, Sonia Sotomayor

#3 Air & Space Museum:

-The pilot was Steve Fossett.   -The plane's ID number:NR7952.

#4 National Archives:

-The inscriptions say: "The heritage of the past is the seed that brings forth the harvest of the future." "Eternal vigilance is the price of liberty."

-The original documents: the *Constitution*, *Bill of Rights*, *Declaration of Independence*.

#6 Museum of American History:

-Francis Scott Key wrote the piece.

-Franklin gave the cane/walking stick to George Washington.

-The name of the exhibit: Woolworth's Lunch Counter, Greensboro Lunch Counter

-The start date of the sit-in: February 1, 1960.

#7 White House:

-The state is Pennsylvania.   -The dollar bill is the 20-dollar bill.

-The President is Andrew Jackson.

-"Zero Milestone" is on the north. "Point for the measurement…" is on the south.

#8 Washington Monument:

The number of flags is the number YOU count.

The decoded date: October 19, 1781.

#9 Korean Vets Memorial: The number: 38; The inscription: "Freedom Is Not Free."

#10 World War II Memorial:

-The number of pillars: 56.   -The words on the arches: Atlantic, Pacific.

-The war lasted from 1941 to 1945.

-The surprise attack was on Dec. 7, 1941.   -D-Day was June 6, 1944.

#11 Martin Luther King, Jr. Memorial:

-The year: 1964.   -King spoke the words in 1968.

#12 Lincoln Memorial:

-The *Emancipation Proclamation* was issued on January 1, 1863.

-Lincoln was assassinated in 1865.

-Lincoln is on the penny and five dollar bill.

#13 Vietnam Vets Memorial:

"Dog tags" (ID tags) hang around his neck.

#14 Jefferson Memorial:

-"Inalienable" and "unalienable" are spelled differently.

-Jefferson was 83 when he died.

#15 FDR Memorial: He led us through WWII. There are 5 statues.

Anytime Missions: The slogan: "Taxation Without Representation"

Note: The information in this book was accurate as of April 2014. We hope that you won't find anything outdated related to the clues. If you do find that something has changed, please email us to kindly let us know. info@ScavengerHuntAdventures.com

58

SCAVENGER
HUNT
ADVENTURES™

We're a family-owned business and
would love to hear from you.

Field trip or group vacation coming up?
Contact us for special bulk pricing and personalized books!

www.ScavengerHuntAdventures.com
info@ScavengerHuntAdventures.com

New York - Paris - London - Rome - Barcelona
Amsterdam - St. Augustine, FL - Washington, D.C.
More on the way!